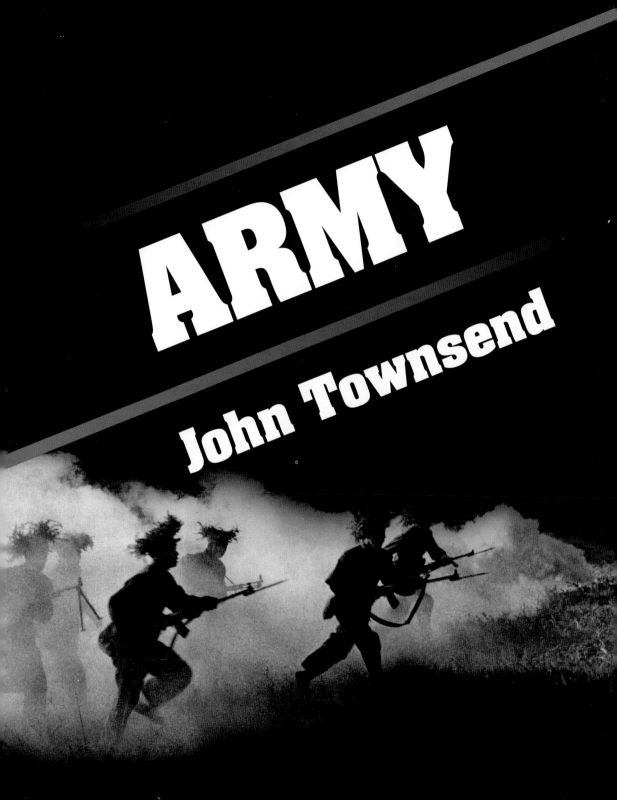

ARMY

John Townsend

A[+]

Smart Apple Media

Published by Smart Apple Media, an imprint of Black Rabbit Books
P.O. Box 3263, Mankato, Minnesota 56002
www.smartapplemedia.com

Published by arrangement with Watts Publishing, London.

Cataloging-in-Publication Data is available from the Library of Congress
SBN: 978-1-59920-982-1   (library binding)
SBN: 978-1-68071-001-4   (eBook)

Picture credits:
The Dimitri Baltermants Collection/Corbis: 12.
Bettmann/Corbis: 10b, 21t, 27.
Central Press/Getty Images: 6.
Cody Images: 8, 9t. 9b, 10c, 13, 25b.
Corbis: 14.
Daily Herald Archive/SSPL/Getty Images: 11c.
Eliot Elisofon/Time Life Pictures/Getty Images: 16b.
Christel Gerstenberg/Corbis: 21b.
Hulton Archive/Getty Images: 1, 18.
Hulton-Deutsch Collection/Corbis: 15c, 29.
Hugo Jaeger/Time Life Pictures/Getty Images: 5b.
LAPI/Roger-Viollet/Getty Images: 7.
Lordprice Collection/Alamy: 22.
Pictorial Press/Alamy: 4.
Picturepoint/Topham: 20b, 25t.
Fred Ramage/Hulton Archive/Getty Images: 28.
Time Life Pictures/Getty Images: front cover.
Topfoto: 19b.
US Army: 19t, 24.
US Office of War: 23.
Wikipedia: 17t, 26.
World History Archive/Alamy: 5t.

Every attempt has been made to clear copyright. Should there be any inadvertent omission please apply to the publisher for rectification.

Printed in the United States by CG Book Printers
North Mankato, Minnesota

PO 1727
3-2015

Contents

Hitler Strikes

Adolf Hitler and his Nazi Party ruled Germany beginning in 1933. By 1939 Germany had the strongest army in the world. Hitler's plan was to take over all of Europe and become the greatest military leader (*Führer*) in the world.

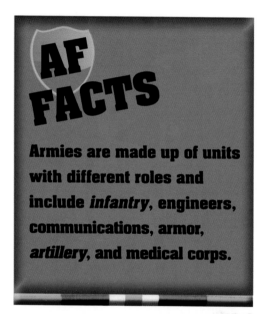

AF FACTS

Armies are made up of units with different roles and include *infantry*, engineers, communications, armor, *artillery*, and medical corps.

On September 1, 1939, Hitler commanded German forces to attack Poland, the country on their eastern border. With their greater strength, training, and equipment, the German Army quickly invaded.

Polish units on horseback were no match for Germany's mechanized forces.

Infantry support tanks during the invasion of Poland in 1939.

Other countries warned Hitler to stop, but he refused. Britain and France declared war on Germany two days later. World War II had begun.

Hitler salutes his German forces in Warsaw, Poland.

Unequal Armies

The German army (or *Heer*) was a well-structured force that had been built over a number of years. The combined armies of Britain and France were no match for it.

The French army had about 900,000 men in 1939. Around 5 million French *reserve soldiers* who received limited military training were soon added.

French anti-aircraft gunners, 1939.

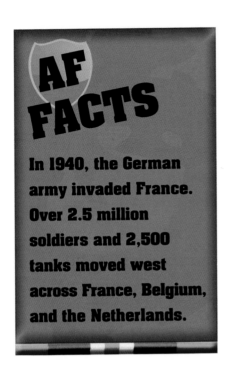
The British regular army had only about 225,000 men. The British brought in *conscription*. By May 1940, the British army had grown to 50 divisions, with 13 of these in France as part of the British Expeditionary Force, fighting the German army along the France-Belgium border.

The Italian army soon supported Germany. By 1940, there were over 1 million Italian soldiers in Libya, North Africa. The British army had just 36,000 men nearby guarding the Suez Canal and Arabian oilfields.

Italian tanks move up to the North Africa battlefront.

Panzer Attack

The invading German army defeated the French troops and forced them and their allies into a tactical retreat. France was now in Hitler's control.

Germany's rapid victories were largely because of new *tactics* used by combining their army, navy, and air force, together known as the *Wehrmacht*. The ruthless, well-organized use of fast Panzer tank forces and infantry units backed by fierce air support was particularly successful. These tactics were called *Blitzkrieg* ("lightning war").

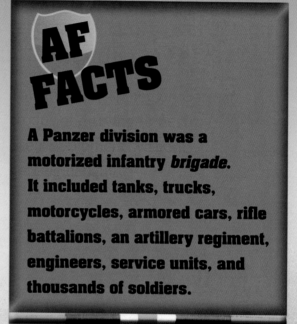

AF FACTS

A Panzer division was a motorized infantry *brigade*. It included tanks, trucks, motorcycles, armored cars, rifle battalions, an artillery regiment, engineers, service units, and thousands of soldiers.

German infantry and Panzers advance during a Blitzkrieg assault.

ACTION STATS

Panzer Kpfw III

This 22-ton (22-t) tank had a crew of five and was the main German tank from 1940–42—a key weapon in the attack on France. It had a 1.5-inch-caliber (37mm) gun and two machine guns. A total of 15,000 were made.

A Panzer Kpfw III in Poland.

Even though the *Allies* joined forces, the Netherlands and Belgium were under German control by the end of May 1940. The German Army marched into Paris two weeks later. Surviving Allied forces fled toward the coast.

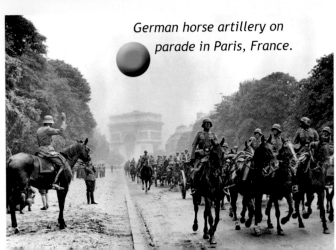

German horse artillery on parade in Paris, France.

Escape: Dunkirk Evacuation

Place: Dunkirk, North France
Dates: May 26, to June 4, 1940
Code name: Operation Dynamo

As the German army advanced across France toward the coast, Allied forces and the British Expeditionary Force (BEF) had to retreat fast, until they could go no farther.

Vehicles and buildings destroyed by German bombing in Dunkirk.

British soldiers make their way through Dunkirk toward the beaches.

Thousands of soldiers were stranded at Dunkirk, pinned against the sea. For some reason, Hitler ordered his advancing army to halt. This gave the Allies time to escape.

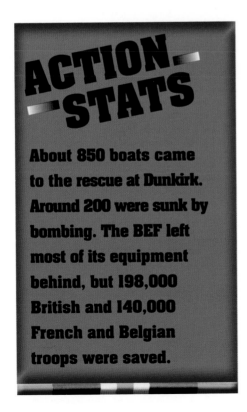

This image from a film captures the chaos that real troops must have faced on the beaches.

About 850 boats came to the rescue at Dunkirk. Around 200 were sunk by bombing. The BEF left most of its equipment behind, but 198,000 British and 140,000 French and Belgian troops were saved.

Back in Britain, anyone with a boat was told to cross the channel to rescue Allied soldiers. It was dangerous, with the German air force dropping bombs all around. German army and naval commanders waited for the order to attack, but it came too late. It was Hitler's first major mistake of the war.

Many escaping soldiers were killed or captured, but hundreds of thousands were saved. Over 220,000 Allied soldiers were rescued from beaches and ports, bringing the total number of Allied troops evacuated to 558,000.

Russia's Army

In 1941, the German army launched an *offensive* against Russia to the east. Named Operation Barbarossa, it was the biggest military operation ever.

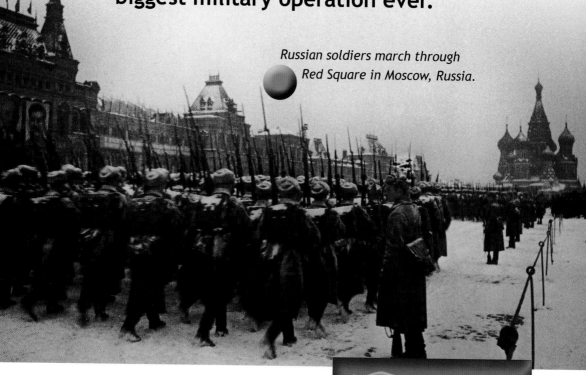

Russian soldiers march through Red Square in Moscow, Russia.

Stalin's Russian army was much bigger than Germany's. It had 24,000 tanks, although only 25 percent worked properly. Despite sending about 3 million soldiers across vast distances to "wipe out" the Russians, Hitler and his army chiefs did not send enough supplies and warm clothing for their army.

AF FACTS

In 1941, Russia's Red Army lowered the age of conscription to 18. (It was 19 for those still in school.)

Under fierce German attack, the Russian army retreated—after poisoning water supplies and burning everything they left behind. All the German army found as it advanced was rubble. That winter was one of the coldest ever and many German soldiers froze to death. Gasoline froze in vehicle fuel tanks. The German army was badly damaged and would never be the same again.

German troops and a Panzer during Operation Barbarossa in 1941.

US Army on the Move

One of the greatest tasks facing any army is moving vast numbers of soldiers and equipment—sometimes across the world.

The USS California on fire in Pearl Harbor.

On December 7, 1941, Japan attacked the US base at Pearl Harbor, Hawaii, which brought the US into World War II. The US Army was *mobilized* for action. Millions of tons of food, weapons, and equipment, as well as millions of US soldiers, were quickly shipped around the world.

US troops land at Casablanca, Morocco, 1942.

Supplies were moved by ship to ports in war zones in Europe, Africa, and the Pacific. Ground transportation was by railway, truck, horse, and even by mule. The US Army was now one of the major Allied forces in World War II.

Desert Battles

During 1942, the Desert War in North Africa saw fierce fighting between *Axis* and Allied forces. At El Alamein, German and Italian armies were defeated by British troops led by Field Marshal Montgomery.

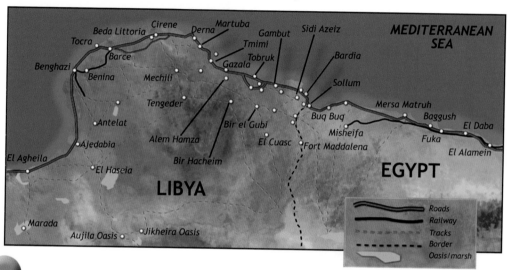

MEDITERRANEAN SEA

Cirene
Beda Littoria
Tocra
Barce
Benghazi
Benina
Mechili
Derna
Martuba
Gambut
Tmimi
Tobruk
Gazala
Sidi Azeiz
Bardia
Sollum
Mersa Matruh
Baggush
El Daba
Fuka
El Alamein
Tengeder
Antelat
Alem Hamza
Bir el Gubi
Buq Buq
Misheifa
El Cuasc
Fort Maddalena
Ajedabia
El Agheila
El Haseia
Bir Hacheim

LIBYA

EGYPT

Marada
Aujila Oasis
Jikheira Oasis

Roads
Railway
Tracks
Border
Oasis/marsh

● Map showing North Africa, with El Alamein on the far right.

An American M4 Sherman tank powering along a desert road.

Tanks were vital in desert terrain, even though they often became stuck in sand dunes or were damaged by heat and dust. Anti-tank weapons such as grenades and landmines disabled many tanks.

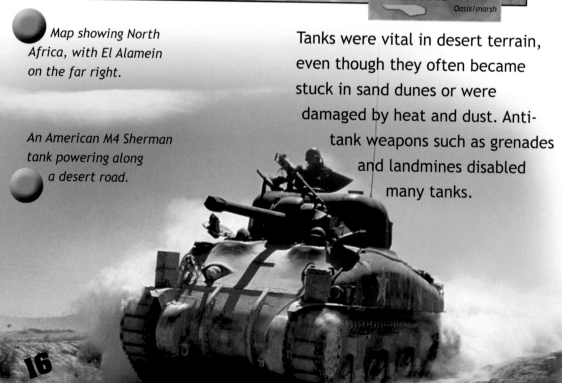

INDEX

About the Author
Holly Cefrey is a freelance writer and researcher.

Australian troops on the front line at Tobruk.

Allied attacks on supplies to Axis camps weakened German fighting power. Their desert leader, Field Marshal Erwin Rommel, had to retreat, against Hitler's orders. At the end of 1942, US-led landings in North Africa helped the Allies take control of the coast. Eventually more than 230,000 Axis troops surrendered to the Allies in Tunisia, bringing the desert campaign to an end.

Jungle Battles

Dense jungles in Asia became battlegrounds in World War II when the Japanese Imperial Army invaded areas and countries around the Pacific Ocean, including Hong Kong, the Philippines, Thailand, Burma, and Malaya.

These places often posed big problems for infantry soldiers because of difficult terrain, such as forests and swamps. Heavy rains (leading to muddy conditions) and dangerous insects or reptiles made conditions even worse.

ACTION STATS

At the start of World War II, the US Cavalry had 12 horse regiments of 790 horses each. The Japanese Imperial Army used hundreds of thousands of horses in combat and for transport.

Japanese soldiers charge into battle.

A column of the 26th Cavalry Regiment (Philippine Scouts), part of the US Army in the Far East.

The 26th Cavalry (US Army) fought the Japanese army in the Philippines. In 1942, allied Filipino-US forces galloped on horseback to capture Morong. Cavalry troops charged and scattered Japanese forces. It was the last-ever combat charge made by US horse cavalry.

World War II was the first war to widely use mechanized vehicles, such as tanks and jeeps, but horses and mules were still used as *cavalry*. In jungle terrain, these animals were often the best way to carry weapons and supplies, as well as taking mounted soldiers to the battlefields.

A Filipino unit uses horses and weapons taken from the Japanese.

Infantry Weapons

Armies on the ground depended on a range of different portable firepower, which included rifles, machine guns, and specialized weapons. Infantry also had access to indirect fire-support weapons, such as *mortars*.

Mortars: A mortar crew usually had at least three soldiers. The gunner controlled the weapon, an assistant gunner loaded the round, and the ammunition man prepared mortar bombs for handing to the assistant gunner.

As well as destroying enemy equipment, mortars were effective for making smokescreens or lighting up enemy lines at night.

Machine guns: Infantry units in all armies worked in squads of about 10 men with light machine guns, such as the British Bren gun or German MG34.

Heavier, tripod-mounted machine guns were used for ground attacks and as anti-aircraft weapons.

A German machine gunner with a tripod-mounted MG34

ACTION STATS

Britain's 3-inch (76mm) mortar was used throughout the war by the British infantry.

- Caliber: 3 inches (76mm)
- Weight: 126 pounds (57 kg)
- Range: 8,400 feet (2,560 m)
- Bomb weight: 10 pounds (4.5 kg)

Flamethrowers: Most armies used portable *flamethrowers* for *bunker-busting* and flushing out enemies. At up to 88 pounds (40 kg), they were heavy to carry, and had a range of almost 165 feet (50 m) with about a 10-second blast.

A Malaysian mortar team, under British command, loads a 3-inch (76mm) mortar.

A German soldier uses a flamethrower to flush out enemy soldiers.

Big Guns

During World War II, heavy artillery included cannons and howitzers with barrels wider than 6 inches (155mm). At the start of the war, many armies had even bigger guns with 8-11 inches (210-280mm) calibers.

A German railway gun fires a shell toward enemy lines.

Artillery weapons were designed to fire explosive *shells* over long distances and cause maximum damage to the enemy.

Heavy artillery guns, such as the German 88 (3.5 inches, 8mm), could be used as an anti-tank and anti-aircraft weapon. Smaller caliber anti-aircraft guns, such as the 1.5 inch (40mm) Bofors gun (right) were lightweight and easy to position.

Making guns and other weapons required more and more steel. People were asked to collect scrap metal to help keep the gun factories going.

BACK 'EM UP WITH MORE METAL

ACTION STATS

The biggest active gun of World War II was the German K5 long-range railway gun which was moved on tracks (left). It fired a massive 562-pound (255-kg) shell up to 39 miles (63 km).

By September 1944, Germany had developed its long-range V-2 rocket. The V-2 flew faster than the speed of sound, with no warning before impact, and had a maximum range of 200 miles (320 km). In 1944, Germany launched over 3,000 V-2s, many across the English Channel to London.

Case Study:
Operation Overlord

Place: Normandy, France

Date: June 6, 1944

Mission: to land 150,000 Allied troops along heavily defended German lines (the largest land-sea-air invasion in history)

Code name: Operation Overlord

The Allied armies could defeat Hitler only by invading France, advancing to Germany, and attacking Nazi headquarters in Berlin. It seemed an impossible task, but by mid-1944 the Allies were ready.

US troops approach the Normandy coast in their landing craft during Operation Overlord.

The Operation Overlord plan, showing the five landing beaches, named Utah, Omaha, Gold, Juno, and Sword.

Troops and supplies on the Normandy beaches, D-Day 1944.

ACTION STATS

Around 6,500 landing craft deployed almost 150,000 Allied forces on five Normandy beaches, while 12,000 aircraft bombed German defenses to provide cover. By the end of August 1944, over 3 million troops had landed in France. About 37,000 were killed.

Operation Overlord, now known as the D-Day landings, began on June 6, 1944. The German army was defending the French coast but didn't expect the landing to be in Normandy. Taken by surprise, German troops were not ready to counterattack with speed and strength. The Allied advance toward Berlin had begun.

Final Battles

Allied paratroopers jump from planes into enemy territory.

AF FACTS

In World War II, paratroopers usually had round-shaped parachutes that could be steered by pulling on four straps. These "risers" connected to the paratrooper's harness and suspension lines, which attached to the parachute canopy itself.

Operation Overlord saw tens of thousands of Allied paratroopers jump from planes into Europe, behind German defenses. Gliders were also used to land troops and equipment.

The troops jumped from planes and landed using parachutes, which took courage and skill. The men overcame German forces and took control of important roads and bridges. This made it harder for the German army to rush extra men to stop the Allied advance.

US paratroopers close in on a farmhouse near the Rhine.

ACTION STATS

During Operation Varsity, over 16,000 paratroopers dropped east of the River Rhine near Wesel, Germany. There were over 2,000 casualties from the two divisions of Operation Varsity, but about 3,000 German soldiers were captured.

On March 24, 1945 the Allies launched Operation Varsity to capture key sites and enable Allied forces to cross the River Rhine. Thousands of British and American aircraft flew nine battalions of the 6th British Airborne Division, and six from the 17th US Airborne Division, toward Germany. It was the largest single airborne operation to occur on a single day in history. It was also the last major airborne operation of World War II.

Defeat and Victory

Russian prisoners of war lift up a US soldier after their liberation in April 1945.

After nearly six years of the biggest battles the world had seen, World War II finally ended on September 2, 1945. Almost 50 million people had lost their lives.

The Russian army reached Berlin in April 1945, a few days ahead of US troops. German forces tried to fight back, but without enough soldiers or equipment, they were overwhelmed. On April 30, Hitler shot himself, two days after the Italian dictator Mussolini was captured and hanged.

Germany surrendered and the Allies celebrated VE Day (Victory in Europe) on May 8, 1945. Japan surrendered three months later on August 15, 1945, signing the official surrender on September 2. The work of the Allied armies changed to helping to rebuild the damaged infrastructure, including railways and bridges. People needed food, shelter, and other supplies—and the army had the resources and equipment to help.

Soldiers from US 7th Army wave flags where Hitler once gave his speeches in Nuremberg, Germany.

29

World War II Timeline

- 1939: September 1 — German army invades Poland. World War II begins.

- 1940: April–June — German army invades Denmark, Norway, the Netherlands, Belgium, and France.

- 1940: June 10 — Italy's army joins the war as a member of the Axis.

- 1940: July 10 — Germany launches air attacks on Britain known as the Battle of Britain.

- 1941: June 22 — Germany and the Axis Powers attack Russia with over 4 million troops.

- 1941: December 7 — Japan attacks Pearl Harbor. The US enters the war on the side of the Allies.

- 1943: September 3 — Italy surrenders to the Allied armies. Germany helps Mussolini escape.

- 1944: June 6 — D-Day: Allied forces invade France and push back the German army.

- 1944: December 16 — German army loses the Battle of the Bulge and the Allies advance on Berlin.

- 1945: April 23 — The Russian army reaches Berlin, followed by the US Army.

- 1945: April 30 — Adolf Hitler commits suicide. He knows Germany has lost the war.

- 1945: May 7 — Germany surrenders.

- 1945: September 2 — Japan surrenders. World War II ends.

Glossary

Allies — countries and armies (US, Britain and its Empire, Soviet Union) that joined forces to fight the Axis powers

artillery — large firearms such as cannon or rockets

Axis — countries and armies (Germany, Italy, Japan) that joined forces to fight the Allies

Blitzkrieg — German for "lightning war": a sudden, violent military attack

brigade — army unit usually made up of four battalions

bunker — an underground defensive fortification, often including a machine gun

caliber — the diameter of a gun's barrel and shells used in it

cavalry — troops mounted on horseback

conscription — being forced to enroll in military service

flamethrowers — weapons that spray fire

infantry — soldiers trained, armed, and equipped to fight on foot

landing craft — a boat specially designed to land soldiers and their equipment on a beach

mobilized — assembled and made ready for action

mortar — short muzzle-loading cannon used to fire shells at a low speed at high angles

offensive — an attacking military campaign (plan of action)

paratroopers — troops trained and equipped to parachute from aircraft

reserve soldiers — civilians who have received some military training and carry out some part-time military duties

shells — metal cases filled with explosives and also sometimes pieces of metal

tactics — carefully planned military actions

Index